LIZZIE BEAUTIFUL

LIZZIE BEAUTIFUL
The Lizzie Velásquez Story

Lizzie & Rita Velásquez
with Cynthia Lee & Lina Cuartas

EPIGRAPH BOOKS
RHINEBECK, NEW YORK

Cover and chapter illustrations by Leslie Rodríguez Alonzo

Book design by Georgia Dent

Library of Congress Control Number: 2010933175
ISBN: 978-0-9825190-0-4

Epigraph Books
27 Lamoree Road
Rhinebeck, New York 12572
www.epigraphPS.com
USA 845-876-4861

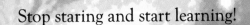

Stop staring and start learning!

Lizzie Velásquez opens her soul and shares her remarkable story, giving us an inspiring testimony. This book, whether read by an individual or shared as a group, becomes a tool to discover that beauty is unique to each of us.

To MY PARENTS whom I adore and strive to be like everyday. To my sister Marina and brother Chris who support me through all of the hard times. To my extended family for their unconditional love. To my friends who help keep my spirits up and encourage me when I'm down. Lastly, to Patty, my special nurse who helps care for me every time I need her.

— Lizzie Velásquez

CONTENTS

ACKNOWLEDGMENT

In honor of all children growing up with long-term medical challenges.

-Dr. James and Janice Lee

INTRODUCTION

L ET'S START WITH some facts about Lizzie. The average 3rd grader weighs 60 pounds.

At 21 years of age, Lizzie Velásquez still weighed that. What's most intriguing is that she doesn't have an eating disorder. Lizzie is one of a handful of people in the world with a rare condition that does not allow her to gain weight. She not only looks unnaturally thin, but her features seem distorted. Also, due to her condition, she has lost sight in her right eye.

Lizzie and her family have faced a lifetime of challenges, living in a society that tends to obsess over outer beauty and perfection. They have decided to share how they deal with the negativity and the challenges that Lizzie still struggles with, day to day. There are valuable life lessons found for us all in her story, which is still unfolding.

Lizzie's mother documented Lizzie's childhood in letters she didn't give her until Lizzie was in college. As you read ahead, you will have a privileged look into this mother's heart and find out more about Lizzie's first years of life.

Lizzie's condition was still undiagnosed at the time of publication.

Lizzie's life story is the starting point for a parable that connects her struggle with any of us; it is the invitation voiced in the title of the last chapter of the book: Fly, Butterfly.

CHAPTER 1

ANGEL BABY

Believe that life is worth living
and your belief will help create the fact.
                                        -William James

WE EACH HAVE an assignment to fulfill.
Every mother provides a cocoon for a precious being. Every baby is enveloped by a mother's body as she patiently nurtures and waits expectantly for the moment when that creature, which has been a part of her own body for so long, will finally emerge into the world.

Have you ever reflected on how pregnancy is an extraordinary course in patience? What a crucial gift that acquired patience will prove to be when parents are confronted by the many challenges posed by bringing up a child.

Rita Velásquez awaited her Angel Baby, nesting and preparing a safe, welcoming home for her baby girl. Her heart was full of hope and eagerness to commit to the care and guidance of her baby, right along with her husband Lupe's constant support. According to all of her pregnancy checkups, she was due to have a healthy little girl.

On Sunday March 12th, 1989, Rita was admitted to the hospital for what she thought were normal labor pains. However, an ultrasound revealed that her baby was in a breach position. To make matters worse, there was also no amniotic fluid left to feed and protect the baby in the womb. The baby girl was alive, which was a miracle, but she had to be delivered urgently.

After an emergency C-section, Elizabeth "Lizzie" Ann Velásquez was born the next day, weighing 2 pounds, 10 ounces. She was 21 inches long. Then, Rita was warned: Lizzie was different.

Rita Velásquez

"I only remember seeing Lizzie the next day in a Polaroid picture because the nurses wanted to prepare me before I went to see her myself.

When I first saw her I kind of got scared and I thought: How can I do this? But then, when they said everything's fine, I thought: okay, she's a baby. I'm okay. I know what to do now."

Lizzie looked below premature. Her parents had to find doll clothes to dress her in because all baby clothes were too big for her. The doctors could not figure out what was wrong and had many fears regarding the baby's health.

Lupe Velásquez

"They said: 'We just have to prepare you. She may be mentally challenged. She may never walk or talk. She'll require services for the rest of her life.' Of course, we listened and respected their opinion. But we had our own. We decided to treat her as normal. We wanted her to be just like all other children."

Doctors expected Lizzie to fail all medical and mental tests. She scored 9 out of 10 on every single one. They also anticipated that Lizzie would be in the neo-natal intensive care unit for three months. The doctors just didn't know what kind of will they were up against. Lizzie was out of the hospital in six weeks.

From the very beginning, Lizzie was labeled as a miracle. She survived a dry womb and managed to disprove the doctor's predictions again and again. Their negatives seemed to be obstacles she was meant to overcome, and just like Lizzie, her parents did not believe all the can'ts and won'ts. From day one, they believed she was an angel who had been sent to earth with a very special purpose, and that she was meant for them.

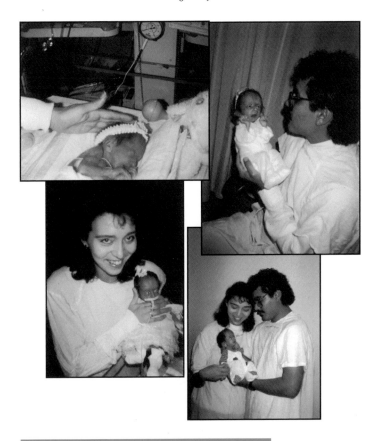

THINK ABOUT YOUR OWN MIRACLES

Have you ever been challenged by what seemed to be impossible?

Do you think that there might have been a hidden lesson in that crisis?

Do you recall any miracles that may have altered the path of your life?

Do you know what your assignment is on Earth?

We All Need to Cocoon Once in a While
Only for You: Create a special place where you can relax and listen to your heart; your very own cocoon.

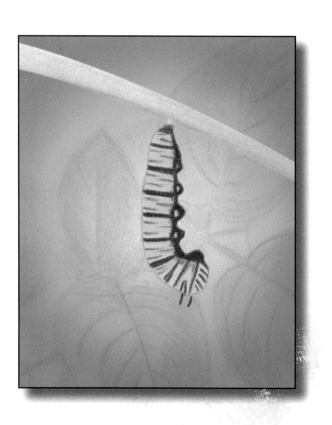

Chapter 2

IT IS WRITTEN

To see a world in a grain of sand
And a heaven in a wild flower
Hold infinity in the palm of your hand
And eternity in an hour.
— William Blake

E ACH DAY, IN itself, brings infinite possibility.
As Lizzie's first months unfolded, her mother Rita kept a detailed journal of Lizzie's development. Rita recorded the food Lizzie ate, the mood changes, her progress and the activities they shared during the day.

Rita Velásquez
"Journaling was very helpful for me. I started after I had Lizzie. When I had to come home without her from the hospital, it was very hard for me. I had been with her in the ICU; knowing that I was going home without her was heartbreaking. I knew that I would be back later that day, but still, I remember holding her tiny little hand and promising her that I would be back and that I loved her so much.

I cried all the way to my room. As I was wheeled out of the hospital, I ran into two other moms who I assumed had delivered the same day. They were leaving with their babies in their arms. I was sitting there holding plants, flowers, balloons and no baby. As we pulled out of the hospital I turned around and watched the hospital disappear as we drove further away.

I returned later that evening with hospital bands still on and walking pretty fast, even though I had had a C-section. I do not remember the pain at all from the surgery. My mind was focused on Lizzie, seeing her and being there for her. The nurses thought I was crazy and did not expect me back that same day. But, there I was, sitting by her incubator, holding her tiny hand and talking to her. I would stay at the hospital until late in the evening when Lupe left his second job to come and get me. Together, we would sit and take turns holding Lizzie's hand, talking to her. At that time, we were not allowed to hold her because she was so small and could not hold her own body temperature. We did this for the first six weeks of her life, driving every day and night to see her. When we were home without her, I would call before we went to bed to check on her and prayed the phone would not ring late at night saying that she was not doing well. I think the hospital only called once or twice.

I started journaling a couple of days after Lizzie was born and still in the hospital. I wrote mainly in the evenings while I was at home. I just found this spiral notebook and started writing my feelings about being scared of not knowing what would happen, and looking forward to the excitement of the day when we would bring her home. Since I was a stay-at-home mom, it was just Lizzie and me all day. While she slept, I would get my spiral out and write about her day.

Journaling allowed me to express myself without her seeing or knowing how scared I was. The more I wrote the more I could feel my fears going away because if something had ever happened to her as an infant, I would have had all these memories in writing as a keepsake. So, writing was my way of dealing with all of this; not knowing if Lizzie would live or not because the doctors did not know her life expectancy. Writing everyday assured me that Lizzie made it another day."

Rita Velásquez

"As for the negatives of the day-to-day with Lizzie, I don't re-member having that many that really stuck with me. When we brought her home, we put a big sign in the yard for all to see that we had a baby girl. We took pictures as we left the hospital with her and then of our arrival at home as we got her out of the car and walked her into her new home for the first time. We dealt with her as any new parents would having a new baby. The only difference was that we could not share her with anyone for a while because her immune system was not fully developed. We were told to be very careful as to who was around her for at least three months. So, we had her all to ourselves for a while which was great. I was very scared of letting her get sick. I think the first time we took her somewhere was to have her baptized at church and boy, was she fussy! I think the noise, the light and the fact that people other than Mom where holding her made her uncomfortable. That was a long day, but she made it and she was so pretty, dressed in her white gown that "ate" her up. We took so many pictures that day just out of pure excitement that we had her out and about. I do not remember if people stared at her or us that day. We were so focused on Lizzie that I did not let it bother me if they did.

Staying home with Lizzie was an easy choice for me. We had decided that she and her health came first. I began taking care of other kids in my home as a way to earn an income and for Lizzie to make some friends. As of today she remains friends with all of the kids I used to watch.

Once in a while, when we would take Lizzie out, some people would stare and point at her, but Lizzie was young and had no clue. We did though. Some people would ask us questions about her, while others would just stare until we stared back and then they would walk off. I do not think I have it in me to be hateful and rude to others so it was very hard for me to confront the people who did this. Her dad is the outspoken one and he defended her to no end. I remember once at the grocery store, I let her walk around while I was developing pictures. A lady walked up to ask me why Lizzie was so small and if she had ever broken any bones. I think she was surprised Lizzie could walk considering how small she was. She shook Lizzie's hand and wished her well."

As the memories unfold, it is remarkable to see that Lizzie went everywhere with Mom and Dad. They have a large, united family that often shares family celebrations and Lizzie was a participant in all of those parties. They attended football games, church functions and Texas festivities, like Fiesta parades. Rita and Lupe made sure their baby girl was right along with them as their daily life ticked along. Lizzie thrived on that constant activity, opportunities to learn, and continuous presence of relatives and friends.

Rita Velásquez

In a letter dated June 4th, 1991

"We went to Toys "R" Us to buy you a bed. We got a pretty white iron bed. It's so small! You loved it. You kept saying: 'Lizzie's bed' and trying to help Dad fix it and help me put sheets on it. That night you slept the whole night in your very own bed. I think your Dad and I stared at you for half the night. We couldn't believe how happy you were."

Lizzie Velásquez

"Going to festivals with my family was one of my favorite things to do when I was younger. There were always so many games to play and all the junk food I could eat. My extended family would be there and just being around them always made everything so much fun. There was always someone to play with who helped keep me entertained. I remember all of us sitting together and watching the parades. I loved watching all the people go by. The floats that threw out candy were even better."

Rita Velásquez

In a letter dated September 2nd, 1990

"Sunday we went to the parade in Waelder (Texas). You looked so beautiful in your sailor outfit. You also rode the horses again and we took pictures. Then, we went to the dance. You danced about five songs with us, then finally fell asleep."

ABOUT YOUR OWN MEMORIES

Have you ever kept a journal? If so, what did you write about?

What do you wish you could remember about your childhood?

If you have children, is there any special way you've tried to capture their childhood?

Do you have a childhood photo album or journal that can help you remember?

Hang a Magic Mirror on the Wall
Only for You: Post your favorite baby picture of you in a special place so that you can easily find the joyful, fearless child inside of you.

CHAPTER 3

A WISE HEART

Never be bullied into silence.
Never allow yourself to be made a victim.
Accept no one's definition of your life;
define yourself.
                                    -Harvey Fierstein

As RITA INHABITED that very special place that Lupe and she created for Lizzie, and as Lizzie grew, steadily accomplishing daily milestones, Rita began to foresee a road full of difficulties. But it was precisely those difficulties that would lead to the happy realization of their hopes and dreams for Lizzie. Rita saw that Lizzie would one day be able to open the journal of memories and understand how much she had been loved. Rita was creating a road back to those cherished moments by using strength and dedication that stemmed from her faith in God and her trust that He knew what He needed to accomplish through her.

Rita Velásquez
      In a letter dated September 10th, 1990
      "You always go to Dad and take his hand to go upstairs. But tonight, I bathed you and you stayed upstairs with Dad while I watched a movie. Dad had even put you to sleep by 9:00pm. It makes me feel great that you spend time with your Dad, but also jealous because you are with him and not with me."

Rita Velásquez
      In a letter dated February 15th, 1991
      "Elizabeth, when you read this journal that I have written for you, it is as if I were talking to you. You will read about all of these memories that are so precious to me: of happy and sad times with you and your Dad and anyone else who comes into our lives. I

know that you will be a very young, beautiful lady and I want you to feel as if I were sitting right beside you, telling you all of these stories myself. I am writing for you, my beautiful and special love-of-my-life young lady."

Sometimes it's difficult for children to truly understand the love their parents have for them until they are parents themselves. Perhaps this bond of affection is the reason for how easily and frankly Lizzie and her family communicate. The relationship between Lizzie and her parents is extremely open, but still, intimate.

This closeness is what inspires Rita to always want to protect Lizzie; even now that Lizzie's an adult.

Rita Velásquez
May 19, 2010
"I took Lizzie to get her nails done and these two very pretty girls walked in. I was already waiting for them to spot Lizzie, which of course they did as Lizzie went to wash her hands. One of the girls was having her nails done and her friend was having a pedicure. As Lizzie walked to the back, they were mouthing to each other across the room with their eyes wide open, saying 'Oh my God.' This whole time Lizzie walked with her head high and paid no mind to them. I, on the other hand, just kept watching. They had not seen me or guessed that I was with her. As I got up to pay, one girl saw me watching her, but kept on mouthing to her friend until Lizzie came to stand with me and she realized that I was with her. She stopped as she was mouthing something and put her head down to look at her magazine as if she had been doing nothing. I could feel my blood boiling and wondered whether I should say anything, or make them feel embarrassed for talking. So, what I did was sit in another chair where, if they turned or looked up and tried to stare at her again, they had to see me first. I sat there thinking: am I sinking to their level or what?

But defending Lizzie will always come first. If Lizzie did notice the staring, she did not show it. I, on the other hand was sitting there like a mother bear just waiting to attack if they moved. How funny is that, I guess I still do this for her at 21 and still feel it is my job to defend her. (Anyway just venting—thanks) That felt good. Maybe I should start journaling again."

As Lizzie grew, Nikki, her cousin and Angelica, her friend, who were both close to Lizzie's age, came to be a part of the daily routine. Rita looked after them and kept them busy and entertained. This allowed Lizzie to have playmates, to learn to share and adapt to not having her mother's undivided attention.

Rita Velásquez

In a letter dated February 1st, 1991

"Nikki is now calling you Lizzie and can even say Elizabeth. She's not afraid to tell on you and Angelica, but it helps because she keeps an eye on you guys. Nikki also knows where the tissues are and whenever she has a runny nose she'll get a tissue and bring it to you so that you can clean her nose. Nikki, Angelica and you are growing so fast and I think that being around each other has helped you all grow even faster!"

Lizzie was surrounded by love.

Rita Velásquez

In a letter dated February 7th, 1991

"You started crying and saying that you were scared. I went to hug you and you seemed to be feeling better. Then, Nikki got up and I put her on the bed with you and you were laughing and talking and hugging each other. Then you decided that you were cold… you kept telling Nikki: 'Hug Nikki,' and you started hugging again."

There were also times for tears, but looking back, they were all shared experiences.

Rita Velásquez

In a letter dated February 15th, 1991

"I had to run to the store for Dad and when I got back you and Nikki were playing in the hallway. All of a sudden, you were screaming and I ran to you and you were covered in washing powder, from head to toe. It was in your hair, in your eyes, your mouth and your clothes. Nikki just stood there, staring and looking very guilty. You just kept on crying and saying: 'Nikki, Nikki.' I asked 'Who did it?' and Nikki said: 'Nikki did.' I just told her to say she was sorry, which she did."

Lizzie Velásquez

"Growing up with Nikki and Angelica, Jelly as we call her, without a doubt contributed to my mentality of not being any different from any other kid our age. They never treated me differently because of my smaller size. Ironically, I was the bully out of the three of us! Whether we were listening to nursery rhymes and playing with toys, painting with water colors, or running around outside, somehow we always got into little fights. But, we still loved each other so much. There is one memory that sticks out the most. All you have to say is 'yellow ironing board' and we all know exactly what that means. On my thirteenth birthday our parents had Nikki, Jelly, and me stand next to each other in front of the TV because they had something to show us. My mom turned on a video and it was the three of us playing and fighting over a yellow ironing board. I had it first and Nikki and Jelly both wanted it. Even though my mom kept telling me to share I kept telling them, in my now famous two words 'three minutes.' Hearing my little mouse voice try to sound so serious and, watching our reactions was hilarious. We loved to play together, but when one of us didn't get what we wanted, there was going to be a fight. Looking back at those days I could not have asked for two better girls to grow up with. Nikki and Jelly have always been there for me, even the birthdays we were too young to remember. Nikki and Jelly made me feel just like they were when the outside world wouldn't. No matter how much older we get or how often we are able to see each other, we will always have a special bond."

There was always a certainty of purpose; relationships that were fed constantly made those years in the cocoon of home a very important stage during which Lizzie developed. There was the confidence and knowledge that Lizzie was loved, accepted and cherished. She knew that she could accomplish anything she set her mind to.

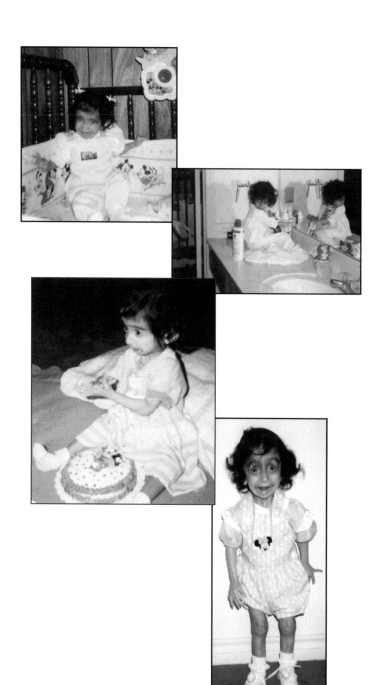

ABOUT YOUR CHILDHOOD

What is your relationship like with your parents and your siblings?

Can you clearly say what you want and what you need?

Do you talk with your friends often?

Who can you turn to when you have a problem?

Your Spider Web
Only for You: Write down the names of anyone who has ever given you a hand when you needed it. They are your spider web of support. Do you need to refresh any of these bonds? Do you need to create new ones?

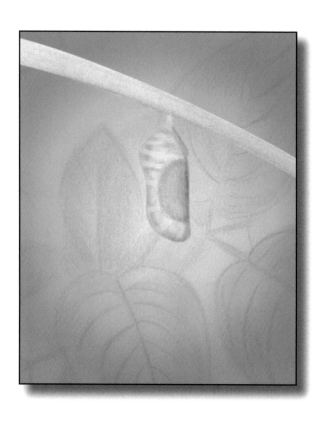

CHAPTER 4

THE FIRST STING

Forgiveness is the answer
to the child's dream of a miracle
by which what is broken
is made whole again,
what is soiled is made clean again.
                    -Dag Hammarskjold

Rita Velásquez

"Lizzie's first day of school was exciting. Lizzie knew the school and teachers because Lupe taught there, so we would visit him a lot. That aspect of school I was not worried about.

What worried me was the fact that Lizzie had not met these new kids in her class and they had not seen her. Lizzie was not a shy little girl and did not know she looked different from other kids her age. The kids whom I babysat were never scared of her and had never called her names or made fun of the way she looked. The environment had been safe at home. Opening this other door was hard and very worrisome for me, but not for Lizzie.

The day before she started school, we had already bought Lizzie the smallest backpack we could find, new clothes and shoes, and made sure she had a bow. Lizzie always had a bow that matched her outfit for the day. She was so excited the night before, talking about all the friends she would make and the teacher, whom she had already met. I was the one worried and wondering what she was going to do if someone said anything about the way she looked. I do not remember talking to her about the 'what ifs.' I did not want to scare her.

The morning of Lizzie's first day she couldn't wait to get dressed, make her lunch and get her backpack ready. Lupe and I walked her to her class together. I remember my heart beating so hard and fast, but I made it seem as if I were under control for her sake. She walked in with a 'good morning' to the teacher. Lizzie then got a book, sat on the floor and waited for other kids to ar-rive. Lupe had to leave because he was still a teacher at that school and had to welcome his own class. So, I was left alone with Lizzie. The bell rang and the teacher said it was time for all parents to leave. I was not ready to go, but Lizzie was fine. She was saying hi to everyone, staying in her spot and looking around. I think I was the last parent to leave. Yet, still, I stood right outside the door, looking in through the glass window, walking off a few steps and going back to the window, then trying to walk off again. I think someone called Lupe because he finally came back down the hallway, told me she would be fine and that he would check on her throughout the day. He took me by the hand and walked me out the door. I made him promise over and over that he would check on her and call. Of course, by lunch he had called and said she was having a hard time because kids were not playing with her. It broke my heart. The next day we went back and I hung out for a while. Lizzie remembered some of the names of the kids in her class and as they came in she told them 'hi.' Little by little, they got used to her and she had a great second day.

Lizzie's years in elementary school were okay. She had ups and downs. Most of the kids remembered her as she moved up in grades. Some kids were mean and made fun of her. When she had bad days she would come home and tell us about it; we would talk and she would feel better, but I think it bothered her. As she advanced in elementary school, her Dad would talk to the class on her first day and explain to the kids – at their level - as much as he could about what was going on with Lizzie, which always made it easier. Lizzie loved it because she was the center of attention and they could ask her questions with her Dad by her side and so she was not scared. By fourth grade though, she did not want to do this anymore, so we followed her lead. When she needed help dealing with anything she knew all she had to do was ask and we both would be there."

Rita Velásquez

In a letter dated May 16th, 1994

"Honey, right now you have had to experience kids at school calling you different names or saying some things about how you look. You tell me a couple of days later and boy, does that break my heart. I really wish that kids wouldn't say those things to you. You are Mommy and Daddy's very special angel and we can't change the way the other kids think or what they say. We can only love you more and be there for you, always. As you go through your life, I am sure that a lot of people will hurt your feelings. Always remember Jesus loves you so much and so do your Mom and Dad, your future brother or sister, all your aunts, uncles, cousins, and grandma and grandpa. Always, always, always remember that."

Lizzie still loved school. She kept up with her schoolwork, despite frequent health issues that made her miss class. Her stomach acted up frequently, she got colds and earaches, and had to have multiple eye exams. Lizzie still thrived and proved to be an excellent student, eager to participate in music, dancing and after-school activities. Mom patiently endured and supported her every way she could, delighting in her successes.

Rita also observed the transformations brought about by Lizzie being around other children. Lizzie wanted to wear clothes like those her friends wore. The discrepancy between the complete acceptance Lizzie found at home and the cruelty in the world outside hurt them all. Still, Lizzie continued to make her best effort growing up. She persevered despite social issues and enjoyed making friends. She managed to show her classmates that she could do anything they could, tried to fit in, and did not give up, no matter how hard things seemed.

Rita Velásquez

In a letter dated April 30th, 1995

"You have been very silly when we go somewhere, especially shopping for clothes. You want to wear clothes like all your friends at school, but you get so mad that the clothes you want don't fit! It's so hard to explain to you that you can't fit into them. We try so hard to get you what you want, but you, my love, are so different. So beautiful in your own special way and I pray so hard every day that life will be great for you, that you can be happy and do not get discouraged by what other people outside our guarded circle might say to you."

Lizzie Velásquez

"I like to think of my elementary years as a big wake up call. Growing up, my parents raised me as a normal kid. I truly had no idea whatsoever that I was different from other people. On my first day of kindergarten I was treated as if I were a monster that nobody wanted to play with. It wasn't until the other kids had such a negative reaction to me that I realized I wasn't like everyone else. I had never had anyone make fun of me before that instance; being accepted and loved was all I knew. Nobody likes to be teased so you can imagine what it was like for a five-year-old girl to have to go through it. I would go home after school and when I would take a bath at night was when I let all the emotions out. The only way I knew how to handle all the pain at that time was to cry. I was so angry at God for making me ugly. I would pray every single night that when I woke up in the morning I would look like everyone else. Every morning when I woke up I was very disappointed. This routine went on for years. As I got older it started getting harder for me to deal with the name calling and stares because I was more aware of why they were doing that to me. I can still hear the names I was called and can picture kids pointing at me while I was walking through the hallways with my class. I was called Skinny Bones, Grandma, Pork Chop Legs, and many other bad names. My first two friends I made in kindergarten were Monica and Lauren.

They accepted me for who I was and ignored what all the other kids were saying. We were the best of friends and they always stood up for me when other kids were picking on me. Once other kids started seeing that I was just like they were, things got easier. I started gaining people on my side and they became like my bodyguards. Every year when I would move up a grade it was always hard because I would have to start over with a whole new class and with kids having to adjust to being around me. I would always get asked the same questions, as to why I was so skinny or why I looked the way I did. There was always such a negative connotation to being called skinny. To this day, I don't like hearing or using that word skinny because it takes me right back to those times. As I got older, I was able to speak up for myself and not let others get to me. I have a very outgoing and friendly personality. Luckily, it worked in my favor and helped me meet new people and let the other kids know that it's okay to be friends. I'm happy to say I am still friends with some of the kids I went to elementary school with. Now that we're all adults, they still tell me if someone is bothering me, they will always have my back. Despite all the hardships of elementary school I learned a lot about myself. Yes, I was born with this syndrome, but it wasn't until elementary school that I was forced to really open my eyes and start learning how to live my life with this syndrome."

Rita Velásquez

"As Lizzie entered middle school it was a whole new ball game for me. The first day I was so worried I thought I was going to be sick to my stomach. I worried about the remarks and the looks since these were kids she did not know. Lizzie was only thinking about the clothes and the right shoes. I had to take her picture in the car because she did not want me taking pictures at school, which I had for all of her first days of school so far. She got out of the car and walked ahead of me with her head up high and walked through all those hot-shot eighth-graders without a second look, while I was behind her, ready to say something. As I watched her go by them, she got looks and second looks, but she just kept on going into the school. She finally told me to leave and that she would be fine. She did have a great day, and year. Middle school was when she decided to become a cheerleader, too. She tried out and made the squad!"

RELATING TO OTHERS

Have you had to endure criticism or teasing?

What is your reaction when people try to put you down?

Does your heart still ache when you think of past hurt?

Focus on Today

Only for You: The best thing you can do if someone has hurt you deeply is forgive and forget. Holding on to your pain can make you bitter and become like a rain cloud in your heart. Forgive all of those people who have hurt you. Write a letter of forgiveness and burn or discard it however you choose. Let your pain go.

Chapter 5

STAND TALL

*A loving heart
is the beginning of all knowledge.*
                    -Thomas Carlyle

L IZZIE AND HER parents have dealt with their share of cruelty. People stare and judge and sometimes ask rude questions or simply ignore Lizzie, as if they felt she had to be feared. People often fear what they can't understand.

Lizzie Velásquez

"Whether I like it or not, I have to face the fact that for the rest of my life people will always stare at me in public though the reasons may differ. Maybe they like the outfit I'm wearing; maybe I've crossed paths with that person before. Either way, I hear that I look different from other people. Between you and me, I just don't see it! In all seriousness I know how society works, you see someone who looks different and you automatically are curious. I'm not afraid to admit that I am the same way. But every stare, every point and every whisper of 'look at that girl' represents a little piece of my inner strength being broken away. This is something that I will live with forever. It's weird because whenever I am stared at in public, I react and feel differently, depending on whom I am with. If I'm out with my friends and people are staring, I always end up laughing. My friends like to turn things around and make the rude people feel uncomfortable. They will either start saying very loudly to make sure everyone around can hear, 'Oh, I hate it when people stare, it's just so rude!' Seeing the sudden look on peoples' faces and then hearing them say, 'Oh, I wasn't staring at her,' and their sudden obliviousness to the whole situation is priceless. Oddly, I'm comfortable with the stares when I'm around my friends because in my mind, people are seeing that I'm a normal college student who is living life and hanging out with people my age. When I'm out with my family and people stare, it is the total opposite. I get embarrassed, not for my family but for myself. I don't like for people to think that I need my parents to stick up for me, even though I know they're doing it because I know it hurts them when people are disrespectful to their daughter. I get this automatic feeling of wanting to completely ignore the whole thing and act like it never happened. When I'm alone and people are staring at me I feel weak. I feel so defenseless. A lot of people ask me why don't I just go up to them and say something. Of course there are times when I wish I could go up to them and scream, 'Stop staring! Leave me ALONE!' My way of handling all of this and rebuilding each piece of my inner strength over and over is simple: I live everyday to the fullest. I continue to live my life every day the way I want to. I make goals and I strive to achieve them no matter what. That is what I tell each and every person who stares, points, and whispers that no matter how long you stare at me, or how you make me feel, I am going to continue to defy the odds."

Lupe Velásquez

"I think by not hiding her or keeping her away from others, we just had her out in public with everyone else. If people had questions we'd talk about it."

Lupe Velásquez

"I always wonder, because Lizzie is so normal to me. I wonder – I wish I could see her from somebody else's eyes so I could see what they see, because she's just a normal child to me. And I wonder what they see immediately."

This natural tendency that causes some of us to judge others by the way they look has to be questioned. We need to evolve as human beings and be willing to allow ourselves to know people on a deeper level. We must open our hearts to the possibility that they are just as human as we are and perhaps have valuable lessons to share.

When people attend Lizzie's speaking engagements they find a heart that has suffered. She has dealt with apparently impossible challenges, but has made the best of what she has been given. She is not focused on her difficulties. Instead, she is making them opportunities to learn more about her strength and resilience. Her generous heart has inspired her to want to share everything she has learned with anyone who is willing to give her their attention and listen to what she has to say.

Pain and suffering are valuable when you learn from their hidden message: you are a glorious human being. Sorrow can compound your heart and plant seeds of empathy and compassion, allowing you to become a beacon to others. If you allow your heart to change, you will find the power and endurance you will need for your earthly pilgrimage and you will learn to see differently, to read beyond differences and enjoy every opportunity to meet others and exchange your stories of life's experiences, both sweet and sour.

Lizzie was willing to push people and stand her ground, even when she was barely two years old.

Rita Velásquez

In a letter dated February 17th, 1991

"When church was over, you told a lady 'bye.' The lady didn't answer, so you said it again and she still didn't answer you, so you yelled 'bye,' with a very loud voice. Dad and I couldn't believe you, but at least the lady told you 'bye,' finally."

LESSONS IN TOLERANCE

What is your reaction when you meet someone who is different from you?

Have you ever caught someone staring at you? How did it make you feel?

Do you go out of your way to help when someone is being mistreated or you witness injustice?

Someone Else's Shoes

Only for You: Try to imagine being someone else. Perhaps think about the life of a woman in Africa, a homeless person living under the bridge, a blind child; there are so many variables to the human condition! Do this exercise and let your imagination help your being grow in empathy and compassion.

CHAPTER 6

OUR UNREAL REALITY

Action and reaction,
ebb and flow,
trial and error,
change - this is the rhythm of living.
Out of our over-confidence, fear;
out of our fear, clearer vision,
fresh hope.
And out of hope, progress.
                              -Bruce Barton

W E ALL HAVE probably been critics, and have also been victims of other's harsh words. We are comparing each other to very unrealistic standards. The most damaging power of this distorted way of looking at ourselves and others is that we slowly interiorize the censorship and become our own worst critics. Do we know what is real anymore?

Angélica Villarreal
"Everybody expects you to be what's on TV and in the magazines. And if you don't fit that image then they question you and look at you weird."

Lizzie has been bombarded by such negativity and there have been idle hands whose best idea to make use of their time was to create websites dedicated to mock and distort Lizzie's photos and stories. This is an expression of fear and ignorance and very little understanding of how we are all interconnected. We still have a lot to learn as human beings.

Lizzie has received hundreds of offensive e-mails from people who say she's ugly. Here are some examples:

Comment: Hey Lizzie! I was just looking at your picture and you are very ugly. How are you a cheerleader?

Comment: The only people that hate you more than me is your parents, because of your syndrome.

Lizzie Velásquez

"The first time I saw the Encyclopedia Dramatica website I was devastated. I knew people had rude things to say about how I looked but never would I think someone would make an entire website not only telling my story but completely bashing me. I read every single word and looked at every picture posted there over and over. The longer I read it the madder I got. It absolutely blew my mind that people who have no clue as to who I really am can be so cruel. They had pictures of my friends, my family and me, and added their own disgusting caption under the pictures. My first reaction at seeing those pictures was guilt. I'm used to people making fun of me, but when they start making fun of my friends and family is when I really lose it. I would rather be called any name in the book or have any bad website about me before I would want someone to say something about the people I care about. In the end, I decided that I must be something special for someone to sit at their computer and make an entire website dedicated to me."

Angélica Villarreal

"Don't judge people as soon as you see them. If I did that and I didn't know Lizzie, I might be scared or nervous to know her, but that would keep me from the gift of knowing her because she's such a great person."

Lizzie Velásquez

"Nobody enjoys having negativity in their life. Unfortunately, it's inevitable whether it's someone criticizing your clothes or something you've done at work or school. In my case, the main source of negativity comes through emails — emails of hate that range from how I should kill myself all the way to saying they would go blind if they saw my reflection in the mirror. Over the years I've saved hundreds and hundreds of emails like this.

I chose to put myself in the public eye and if receiving these nasty emails is part of it, then so be it. Why not turn those emails into something positive? I'm the type of person to whom if you say I can't do something I will do everything in my power to prove you wrong. This is where the emails come in. Every time I read one of those hateful messages I get so angry. The words on my computer screen feel as if someone is reaching through and kicking me while I'm down. At the same time, I look at these emails as one big game of truth or dare. People say I won't amount to anything or I should never leave my house. In my mind I'm thinking, dare me. Dare me to leave my house and watch me prove you wrong. Dare me to live my life how I choose and watch what I really can amount to. I save every single disgusting email because once I accomplish everything I want in life and maybe even more, I can look back at those emails and think: who's the one laughing now?"

Lizzie Velásquez

"Finding the videos of me on YouTube entitled the Worlds' Ugliest Woman was another one of my low points in life. The first video I saw, I bawled my eyes out. There were millions of hits on this one video and thousands of comments posted. I sat at my computer reading all the comments and cried like someone was physically hurting me. People were referring to me as an it and saying they lost their appetite after looking at me. Honestly I don't understand how people could be so heartless. After a while the tears stopped and the anger settled in. With my mom's help we did successfully get a couple of videos taken offline only to have an email sent from one person telling us we hadn't won and that he was going to just post it again. After reading that email my fingers were ready to hit the keyboard and type him a message that would hurt him just as bad as he hurt me. I was ready to set this guy straight and also reply to all the comments posted to the video. I soon realized that even if I typed a message to fight back I really wasn't going to accomplish anything. No matter what I would say they could still post another video of me or reply to me and make me feel even worse. Arguing with these ignorant people would just make me sink down to their level. It would turn into a battle that would never end. Believe it or not, I want those people to keep saying bad things about me. Those people can stay behind their computers and I will continue to do more things in my life than they probably ever will."

Lizzie Velásquez

"Music is my best friend when it comes to keeping a good attitude. I can put my iPod on shuffle, turn it up loud and the perfect song always plays. Whether it is a fast, upbeat song or a slow inspirational one, my spirits are always lifted. There are some songs I'm convinced were written about my life. Listening to a song that I can relate to seems to be the answer to any problem. Spending time with my friends also keeps a smile on my face. I don't have to worry about them judging me because of my looks or afraid to touch me because I'm small. I can be myself around them and I love that. Hanging out with my friends is like me charging my batteries. After being around them I feel completely happy, confident and strong, like I can take on the world. Music, friends, and laughter are what make me one very happy girl."

Lizzie's favorite songs: "It's Your life" by Francesca Battistelli, "Hope Now" by Addison Road, and "More Beautiful You" by Jonny Díaz.

YOUR OWN TAKE ON REALITY

Is there something that has always bothered you about yourself?

Have you ever made fun of someone?

Has anyone ever made fun of you? How did it make you feel?

How can you soften your heart and open your eyes to a gentler way of looking at people?

An Answer to Negativity
Only for You: Defend your thoughts about yourself from the standards you are bombarded with by the media and others. Look at the people around you! Listen to the stories they want to share. Block your negative streams of thought and remember to look in the mirror and tell yourself that you love yourself, just the way you are, at least once a day.

CHAPTER 7

MEDICAL MYSTERY

It is not length of life,
but depth of life.
          -Ralph Waldo Emerson

THE QUEST TO find out what exactly Lizzie has persists. No doctor has been able to figure out what causes her body to block the processing of fats, hardening many of her body tissues. This condition also causes her to have problems with several of her body systems. Lizzie already lost vision in her right eye, has problems with her hearing, her bones and cannot gain weight. She has been referred from doctor to doctor. No one can accurately identify her syndrome.

Rita Velásquez

In a letter dated April 9th, 1991

"We showed him (genetic counselor) what we had and he said almost exactly what we already knew. I guess I was expecting to hear something different. Your Dad just didn't like him at all. His exact words were:'he was full of a lot of hot air.' Well, all we can do is to try and that's what we are doing."

Rita Velásquez

"When we first started with the genetic specialists I read everything they gave me and looked up what I did not understand on the web. Many things scared me to death, such as what her life expectancy would be and what could happen to her as she grew. Many times after reading these articles I would be in tears wondering: IF she had this, or what were we going to do. Well the 'ifs' became too much one day. I put all the paperwork aside and told myself to live one day at a time and to leave it in God's hands. I reminded myself that He gave us this blessing and it was all under

His control, not the doctors' and that He would carry out His will with her. Accepting this has done wonders for me and my sanity. Now, I take all the what ifs with a grain of salt and believe that Lizzie will surpass whatever comes her way. Today, we, or I should say Lizzie, has decided that she no longer wants to be poked and looked at by different doctors anymore. So right now, we see one doctor in Dallas that has done studies on her and has been keeping track of her for several years. We are still trying to find the gene that caused whatever is going on with her."

Lizzie has met two other girls with characteristics that resemble her condition. One lives in England, the other in Texas. Lizzie is the smallest out of the three and perhaps the most outspoken.

Rita Velásquez

In a letter dated February 26th, 1991

"The genetic disorders specialist was very interested in you, as is everyone who meets you. Your Dad and I are trying to get you to see him just in case he can see something that the other doctors haven't seen. One thing your Dad and I have agreed on is that no one will do any more poking or things that will hurt you to explore. Liz, I hope that when you are old enough to be reading this and all the other things that I have kept for you, you will understand all of this was done to help you, and us, understand what has happened to you since your birth."

At one point, doctors thought Lizzie had DeBarsey's syndrome, but that was finally ruled out.

Rita Velásquez

In a letter dated January 2nd, 1992

"The genetic specialists have finally labeled you with De Barsey syndrome. To Mom and Dad, you are just Elizabeth, our beautiful and wonderful little girl. The only sad part of this syndrome is that we cannot give you a brother or sister. But we are trying other options and considering adoption as well. There are days when I'm down and wish this would have never happened, but most of the time I don't even think about it and I'm just very, very grateful to have you."

Some experts believe that Lizzie's condition is a type of lipodystrophy and that is why she looks like patients who have this syndrome. According to the medical definition of lipodystrophy, it is any disturbance of fat metabolism. This general category could definitely include Lizzie's case. However, when biochemical factors and more specific symptoms are studied, the precise nature of Lizzie's condition remains a mystery. One of the differences is that lipodystrophy sets in during childhood, causing the appearance of the face and upper limbs to thin dramatically, often irreversibly. These cases also have skin lesions that are crucial for diagnosis. Lizzie's symptoms have existed since birth, and her clinical evolution does not conform to any known and recognized syndrome.

Lizzie still hopes her condition, when diagnosed, will be named Lizzie's Syndrome. Moreover, since there is no prognosis, no one knows how long Lizzie will live.

Lizzie Velásquez

"Anytime I have a major medical setback such as unexpected emergency surgeries or hospitalizations, I never think: this could be it. Thinking about my life expectancy is honestly something that doesn't cross my mind. Whenever I'm sick, my mind and body automatically go into fight mode. Not getting through whatever it is, it's just not an option. No matter how serious my illness may get, I never get scared. I have only had one really close call with death. After unknowingly losing half the blood supply to my body, I was hospitalized for a major blood transfusion. Once I received the transfusion and was doing a lot better, it started to dawn on me that I had been very blessed to have not only made it to the hospital on time, but to be given a second chance. Since that day,

I have always told myself never to worry about dying. Life is so precious and I don't want to waste any minute of it worrying when it will be my time to go. Instead, I wake up every morning ready to take on the world."

Despite what doctors told Rita and Lupe, they went on to have two healthy children who do not share Lizzie's syndrome.

Lizzie Velásquez

"The fact that my younger siblings do not have my condition has never bothered me. I'm actually grateful that I am the one living with it. There are a lot of unknowns and medical issues that I have to go through and I would never want any of my family members to deal with the hardships of living with this condition. The fact is, I have to see many doctors, have a lot of surgeries, and deal with the repercussions of having a weak immune system. All of that takes a toll on my body and it leads to a lot of absences from school and basically having to put my life on hold. I want my siblings to be able to continue living the wonderful healthy lives that they do now and I will gladly be the one who has to endure the tough days."

As for Lizzie having children of her own someday, doctors say since her body functions normally like any other woman, she is capable of conceiving.

Rita Velásquez

In a letter dated November 6th, 1993

"Hopefully, one day all of our questions will be answered. And I promise, we won't give up until they are all answered."

YOUR OWN MYSTERIES

Do you frequently doubt your own perceptions and ask for advice from others?

Can you read your body's responses to situations?

Do you follow your gut feelings?

Is there something you had wanted to know for a long time and then finally found an answer?

Taking Care of All of You

Only for You: You are made up of your mind, body and soul. If you are familiar with prayer and silent contemplation, you can also try meditation. Meditating simply requires slowing down your breath, closing your eyes and whether with a guided imagery, or by yourself, find the way to the space of absolute peace inside of you. You can start with short periods of meditation, and increase the time as you feel more and more comfortable in this peaceful state. Meditation has proven to relieve pain, increase self-esteem and contribute to diminishing stress and depression.

CHAPTER 8

THE THREE F'S

In everyone's life, at some time,
our inner fire goes out.
It is then burst into flame
by an encounter
with another human being.
We should all be thankful for those people
who rekindle the inner spirit.
                    -Albert Schweitzer

Lizzie Velásquez

"I got my charm bracelet on my seventeenth birthday. I had wanted a charm bracelet for awhile, but little did I know how special it would become to me. Every charm I get has its own special meaning. My bracelet represents so much more than just a simple accessory. To me it symbolizes love and the special relationship that I share with whoever helps add onto my bracelet. The first charm I received was the number 17. My second charm, also given to me for my birthday, was a butterfly. My parents gave me a guardian angel charm. Knowing the reason why someone bought the charm specifically for me is so much more personal. I am a self-admitted daddy's girl and having that charm on my bracelet is very special to me."

Lizzie's shield of armor has always been composed of her three F's: Friends who love and support her, her Family who have always been there beside her, and her Faith, which not only feeds her soul, but literally follows her wherever she goes.

Lizzie Velásquez

"Throughout my entire life my friends and family have made me feel so loved in so many ways. One of the things I love about being in a big family is all of our family get-togethers. I wouldn't have it any other way. I look forward to holidays because when everyone is together it makes me so happy to be surrounded by love and laughter. It's the little day-to-day things that keep me so upbeat like a simple text message that asks how I'm doing. Or, a message wishing me a good day. I'm able to talk with my friends about anything and everything. Sometimes, the fact that they are just there to listen to me vent or to have a shoulder to cry on makes me very grateful to have them in my life."

People from Lizzie's church attend her speaking engagements and have rallied behind her since she was a child. They see her as an angel, a messenger of love and light.

Lizzie Velásquez

"Being told I'm like an angel is one of the biggest compliments. I feel so honored. At times I don't feel worthy enough to be thought of so highly because in my eyes I'm just a regular girl. Firefighters, policemen, and soldiers in my opinion are the angels here on Earth who help protect and save lives daily. There are occasions, however, when I do feel like it is my duty to be God's messenger and spread the good word. It can be a very big responsibility to take on such a task, but simply putting forth the effort to share my message can be so powerful in itself."

It was precisely at church that Lizzie had her first experiences in front of a crowd. She was a lector, taught 2nd grade Sunday school, sung in the choir, participated in Christmas pageants, and still participates in church functions today.

Lizzie Velásquez

"My faith is what has gotten me where I am today. I was raised in the church and grew to love and learn more about my faith as I got older. Throughout my life there have been so many instances where I felt like God was giving me a sign or a little nudge of confidence. On my 15th birthday, I went to my confirmation retreat with all of my friends from church. We were all expecting to have a boring weekend. We were in the middle of nowhere, our cell phones had been confiscated, and there were bugs everywhere. After the first session of prayer and activity, things started looking up, perhaps a sign that maybe the weekend wasn't going to be so bad after all. Throughout the rest of the retreat I felt like my body was being taken over by the Holy Spirit. The amount of joy and excitement I had in my heart was overwhelming. Despite there being a big group of teenagers there, I felt like God had called me to that specific retreat. The timing couldn't have been more perfect. I had just given my first big speech and the thought of becoming an inspirational speaker was already on my mind. That weekend was the confirmation and reassurance that God's plan for me is to not only spread my story, but to be a light in this world.

There are many Sundays I can remember where I either didn't want to wake up early to go to church or I was just in a bad mood that day. But it would never fail, as soon as I walked out of church I was singing the praise and worship songs all day and my mood would be completely changed. I would feel re-energized and so pumped up to share my story because I knew it was what God wants me to do. Knowing I'm following the path He wants me to take is the greatest blessing I could ever ask for."

Rita Velásquez

In a letter dated September 17th, 1993

"God has given you a lot to deal with, but Honey, always know that He has a reason and know that He loves you and will always watch over you."

FAITH, A PERSONAL MATTER

Is prayer part of your daily routine?

Do you remember to think about all the blessings in your life often and to give thanks for them?

If you had a charm bracelet, what would be on it?

A Shield of Armor
Only for You: Design your own shield of armor. What are the essentials in your life that create a protective support system? You can envision it as a bracelet, a pendant, or an emblem, like a coat of arms, that summarizes the strongest components of your life and which help you navigate difficult times.

CHAPTER 9

NO SECONDS

Who looks outside, dreams;
who looks inside, awakes.
-Carl Jung

Lizzie Velásquez
"To a lot of people I am Lizzie, the girl who despite all the odds is so strong and has so much courage to get through every day despite the downsides of having a rare syndrome. Yes, I do try to make that my reality, but to be honest, I sometimes feel like I'm hiding behind my smile. There are days when I feel like the whole world is against me. Just like any other girl, I have my bad hair days and days when I'm just in one of those moods. But there are also days when I get so angry because my jeans look like they can fit one more person in them. There are also the days when being blind in one eye is so frustrating because I have to work overtime with my good eye. Those are just the little things though. There are only two times in my entire life that I can remember when I felt like I completely lost it; lost the pride I had in who I was, the courage to say it's okay to be different and lost the strength I carry in my heart.

It was a regular school night, I was in my dorm room sitting at my desk distracting myself from homework and listening to music on YouTube. I was in a really good mood, laughing and talking with my roommates when I noticed something familiar on the right side of my computer screen. It was a link to one of my bad videos online.

I've seen the video a million times and have read a lot of the horrible comments. I don't know why, but I clicked on the video and started reading the comments again. For some reason it was like seeing the video for the very first time. Reading the comments hit me like a ton of bricks. I felt the tears start welling up in my eyes. Right when I started crying my phone rang and it was one of my best friends. He noticed I was upset and asked if I wanted to take a walk. I left my room and made sure my roommates didn't see me upset. I don't like people seeing me get upset about negative things that happen to me because of the way I look. I always think I have to be some type of superwoman and not let bad things affect me. I felt like I was having a breakdown. I was crying so hard, the kind of crying where you can't catch your breath. I was so tired of people judging me without knowing me, angry at the fact that no matter where I go people won't leave me in peace and have to make me feel like I'm something out of a horror movie. We went into a room in the student center and I was just venting and crying like there was no tomorrow. I didn't want to have to put on a brave face anymore. So many things were going through my head. It felt like we were in that room for hours. After a good long talk with my friend, he helped me remember why I was put on this Earth and the message that I was meant to spread. It was as if the light switched on again and I knew I needed to snap out of that awful mindset I was in. To this day, I remember exactly how I felt and what I went through that night. I use it as a tool to help remind myself of my purpose and the reason I must always keep my head up high and truly believe, love, and cherish who I am."

Lizzie Velásquez

"I would never change what I have lived through because of all of the opportunities, all of the lives I'm being able to change now. I don't feel like I'd be able to do that if I didn't look the way I did."

Lizzie Velásquez

"It took many years for me to be able to look in the mirror and truly like what I saw. Having to go through adolescence is hard enough, but to have to deal with the media's idea of a 'pretty girl' on top of looking completely different from other girls was one of the biggest obstacles. It was so frustrating because if I changed the way my hair looked or bought the new clothes that everyone was wearing, I still didn't look like the other girls. I like to think of it as my Jan Brady phase. She did everything in her power to wash the freckles off her face, but no matter how hard she scrubbed, the freckles were always there. That's exactly how I felt. No matter what I did, my looks never changed. My sophomore year in high school was when I first really started to like who I was in my own skin. One day it just clicked in my head and I realized I was made like this for a reason. I wasn't going to be able to wish upon a star and wake up looking like everyone else. I figured I might as well make the best of it. Every time I looked in the mirror and thought something negative about myself, I would stop myself. Now that I am 100% comfortable in my own skin, I feel happier and a lot more confident. There are going to be days when I do get frustrated with my looks, but in reality, what girl doesn't?

With as many struggles and obstacles that are thrown my way, I've learned to always find the humor in any situation. If I didn't, I would always be upset and nobody wants to be around a Sad Sally! My Dad knows how to make me laugh, even when I don't want to. He says, 'If I count to three and you don't smile that means you're really mad.' By one, I am already full of smiles. There has never been one single time I haven't smiled or started laughing when he says that and it makes me even madder. Whenever I'm in the hospital recovering from a surgery, he is the first one to make me laugh despite all the pain. I used to tell him not to make me laugh hard because I was convinced a stitch or staple would pop open. Laughter to me is the best medicine. There are often times when the last thing I want to hear is something funny, but it's hard for me not to find the humor in a situation even if I'm in the worst mood. I'm really quick on my feet when it comes to making someone laugh or even laughing at myself. I'm able to make light of my situation and when others see that, it makes them feel comfortable because they know that I don't take myself too seriously. I told one of my friends that the shirt he was wearing brought out his eyes. He in turn said mine did as well. My immediate reaction, 'Thanks! But which eye?' I mean, after all, I do have one brown eye and one blue eye so he could've been talking about either one!"

Today, when you view videos of Lizzie, you will see her sense of fun is still growing. There are pictures of her at the beach, in a bikini of course, having fun with her friends under the sun. She goes to dances, on road trips and plays Twister with the rest of the gang. You will find her on a see-saw, trying her luck at the hoola hoop, dancing and shopping with friends.

Lizzie Velásquez

"I have a love/hate relationship with shopping. Don't get me wrong; it's definitely a lot more love than hate. Ever since I was little, dressing up was one of my favorite things to do. Whenever I go out, I always have to make sure the outfit I'm wearing is just right. In my opinion, people are always going to be staring at me, so why not give them something to look at. Finding clothes that fit, on the other hand, is a whole different story. I don't have any favorite stores. Whatever store I find that has clothes that I like and that actually fit my tiny body, I love. Often I go into a store in a very eager mood to shop, but when I find something I really like and it's either too big on me or they don't have my size, I'm not a happy camper. I still fit into a lot of kids' clothes and trying to find shorts or even shoes without flowers or cartoons on them is difficult. Jeans are the hardest to find. My parents found a store recently that carries size triple zero. Yes, we hit the jackpot! I recently started buying skinny jeans; I don't know why I didn't think about buying those a long time ago, maybe just because of what they are called. I have three pairs of them and they fit like a glove. Even with the difficulties of finding clothes that fit, I still enjoy shopping. It's one of my favorite hobbies.

When I'm not out spending all my money, I love to be with my friends. No matter what we're doing or where we are, we always have a great time. I think if you left us in an empty room we would still have a blast. You can either find us watching movies, hanging out around campus, or sunbathing by the river. Since I've been in college, I've had a lot of spontaneous trips with my friends. One minute we're lying around bored and the next we're packing up and going camping. We've taken lots of road trips to each other's hometowns just for a little getaway.

We also love to eat! Let me just say I am probably the pickiest eater you will ever meet. I will eat chicken fingers, fries, pepperoni pizza, or grilled cheese any day. At some food places around campus, the people working there already know what I'm going to order when they see me in line. Some of them even give me extra food! They probably took one look at me and thought I needed it. My friends are always telling me it's not fair, but you sure won't hear any complaints from me."

Rita Velásquez

"Lizzie always loved to wear bikinis when she was younger. Her first bathing suit was this tiny, little, lime green one, trimmed in black with a zipper in the front. This suit was so small, but it fit her perfectly. As Lizzie got older, she preferred the two-piece suits. Many times I had to sew the suit in order for it to fit. Lizzie was very comfortable in bikinis and had no insecurities about being in them, unlike most teenagers. I, as her Mom, always knew she would be stared at because she was so thin, but Lizzie was just fine. I think we did a good job on building her self-esteem and never let her feel as if she looked different from anyone else, even though we knew she did. That might be why she is very comfortable in her own body and has never been worried what others might say. I feel sad when people stare at her because they do not know her; they don't give her a chance and just judge her based on her appearance. If they only knew what a great kid she is!"

The only thing that can make Lizzie stay still is her health. But any other day, she is out in the world, unwrapping each experience as if it were a gift, and finding the fun that complements the other 3 F's in her life.

FINDING YOUR OWN FUN

Do you remember what your favorite game was as a child?

Is it easy for you to find humor in daily situations?

Do you believe that life gives us second chances?

What have you always wanted to do and never dared to try? Make a purpose of at least trying your luck at it!

Your Fun Can

Only for You: Make a list of things that you love to do, perhaps, reading a favorite book, ice skating, scrapbooking, painting with watercolors, playing soccer, or rowing on a lake, and cut them out into individual pieces of paper. Put them in an empty can and when you are having a blue day, treat yourself to a fun date.

CHAPTER 10

BEYOND THE COCOON

Teach me to wait patiently,
while my wings grow strong.
For my time to fly has not yet come.
　　　　　—Sue Monk Kidd
　　　　　When the Heart Waits

Lizzie Velásquez

"When I lie awake at night, I imagine what my future could look like. For as long as I can remember, I've always had my heart set on becoming a motivational speaker, writing a book, graduating from college with a master's degree in communication studies, and having a family of my own. Who would've thought by the young age of 21 I'd already be able to mark my top two goals off my list. As I've pursued my college degree, my eyes have been opened to so many things. Learning the tools to help build my career has made me think about what I really want my future to look like. I want to one day be able to find that special someone to love me for who I am. I dream of finding someone who would be able to look past my syndrome. Just like every girl, I want the fairytale wedding with all the works! Without a doubt, I want to start a family and hopefully even be supermom just like my mom. I would also love to travel around the world. There are so many cultures and so many different people; I would love to be able to experience it all. Twenty years from now I want to look back at my life and hope that all these things came true. Some of my dreams and goals may change along the way; I can't wait to see how it all plays out."

Deep down inside, Lizzie has always wanted to find a way to get noticed by people with the right connections so that she could have a platform to share her message with the world. She went to college at Texas State University with the goal of becoming a motivational speaker.

Lizzie Velásquez

"I am willing to talk to anyone who will listen to me. If I speak to a room full of 1,000 people and I affect the life of one person, that's all that matters to me."

Lizzie has already been on TV. She even started a petition to try to get on the Oprah Winfrey Show. Still, nothing seemed to work in the beginning. Interestingly, Lizzie finally got noticed when she stopped trying to make things happen the way she thought they should unfold. Lizzie decided to just focus on her college schoolwork.

Lizzie Velásquez

"Whenever I set my mind to something, I create a sort of competition with myself. When I set my sights on something, I feel like I have to find a way to complete it or else I get aggravated that I didn't follow my plan through. I have had many obstacles thrown my way, but with most things I always try to turn the negative into a positive. Let's say I want to learn how to write in another language, but in the process I have an accident with my right hand. Of course you'd think, 'well that's that, I'll try another time.' That's just not something I would settle for. I would teach myself to write with my left hand just to prove to myself that I can fulfill that goal. I have to admit I can be very stubborn, but in this case, I think it helps to make me determined in everything I do."

Right before Lizzie's junior year in college, a professor from her university told the founder of Motah, LLC (an inspirational website) that Motah should feature Lizzie.

Motah (pronounced 'mō-də for motah-vation) did a video story on Lizzie, posted it online and networked it. Within a month, television producers from Los Angeles, New York and London had all made contact interested in producing a TV documentary. Within a year, Lizzie was featured on NBC's Today Show.

Lizzie Velásquez

"I've always been told things happen when you least expect it. I can say without a doubt, I believe that now more than ever. The morning I got the call about the *Today Show*, I woke up and was planning to be in my pajamas all day, studying for my philosophy class. Little did I know that one phone call would lead to the gates of my dreams opening up. When I answered the phone, heard the lady say hello and tell me who she was and why she was calling, my heart sank to my stomach. I had to keep telling myself, 'calm down Lizzie, calm down!' The moment I hung up, I stood in the kitchen and let it all sink in.

Once I realized how huge this moment was I got so excited, I wanted to jump and scream. The only problem was, I was home alone at the time, so I picked up my puppy Bitsy and was telling her what phone call I had just received. Even though she just stared at me with her little puppy eyes, I knew she was jumping for joy with me deep inside. I called my parents straight away expecting them to answer, but neither of them did and I was going crazy! Once I finally got a hold of them they didn't believe me and thought I was joking. They finally realized that this was really happening and it was a moment I will never forget."

No matter how badly we want to run, we need to crawl and walk first. Life involves processes that develop in us the skills that we will need to excel at what we long to achieve. And these dreams are not only ours, they have been planted by a power greater than we are that wants us to succeed. He needs us as His instruments.

BREAKING THE COCOON

Do you find it hard to let go of control?

Have you experienced getting what you want as soon as you stop trying?

Do you worry about your future?

Do you take the time to listen to people around you and be observant of your environment? Very often chance encounters or overheard conversations can have clues or provide ideas that can help us get what we want.

*Be vigilant. Tune into the flow of life and the tools you need to build your dream will come your way.

The Gift of Today
Only for You: Indulge in your routines. They are yours to relish, yours to delight in. Look around you, in nature, at how many of God's most beautiful creations require processes, evolution, and waiting. The rose lived as a bud before she unfurled in splendor, an oak tree was first a tiny seed before it grew even one leaf, animals take their time to grow in size and might. And each stage has its purpose, its magic, its power. Rejoice in who you are today, what you can do, and the thrill of being alive!

CHAPTER 11

FLY, BUTTERFLY

Just living isn't enough,
said the butterfly.
One must also have freedom, sunshine
and a little flower.
—Hans Christian Andersen

Lizzie Velásquez

"My mission on Earth is to help anyone who feels that they are different. I want to help the people who have obstacles in their life and need that extra help to overcome them. Having someone to relate to is such a tremendous help and I want to be that person people can look at and think: if she can do it, I can too. I will work towards that goal everyday that I am alive. Some people may look at me as an angel sent to teach society a lesson. But what's the lesson? My lesson is simple. Don't let others' opinions of you keep you from doing whatever you set your mind to. Let the negative people try to bring you down because it will only make you stronger in the end. Fight to be the best person you can be and never let your differences hold you back from reaching for the stars. The possibilities are endless."

Fly, Butterfly
Against the impossible
Against the wind
With the breeze of faith,
With the waves of change,
Soar, glide, fearlessly.
Let the loving currents carry you.

Lina M. Cuartas

Lizzie appears on the *Today Show*, July 2010

Lizzie Velásquez

Lizzie has already embarked on a career as a motivational speaker. She is very involved in her community and church. Lizzie has volunteered with the Hispanic Mother Daughter program, taught in high schools, and visited with nursing home patients during the holidays. She looks forward to traveling the world and sharing her story. Visit www.aboutlizzie.com for more information.

Rita Velásquez

Proud of her daughter, Rita continues to support Lizzie in everything she does. A former childcare giver, she is currently a receptionist for her church parish. Musically gifted, Rita is also the coordinator of church choirs and plays the guitar.

Cynthia Lee

Cynthia Lee is a former television news anchor who left the business to broadcast all positive news on her website www.gomotah.com. After 12 years in T.V., Cynthia created Motah (pronounced 'mō-də for motah-vation) where you can upload your own inspirational videos. She is also a philanthropist and raises money for various non-profit organizations.

Lina Cuartas

Lina Cuartas is a published author and artist from Colombia. Through her experience living in the Amazon rainforest, she instituted a learning program for children in Colombia, and wrote two books: *Come Grow with Me* and *Come into My World!*.

LaVergne, TN USA
22 September 2010
198025LV00001B